IMAGES
of America

CATHOLIC BOSTON

A Holy Name Society parade winds its way down Stuart Street in Boston when the city hosted the society's national convention in October 1947. Groups from all over the Northeast participated, including the society's branch from Providence College, seen here. In the large building at right is the former Burdett College, also known as Burdett School of Business; the school name can be seen printed on the windows. (Courtesy of the archive of the Archdiocese of Boston.)

ON THE COVER: This 1930s photograph shows Card. William Henry O'Connell, archbishop of Boston from 1907 to 1944, processing down the center aisle of the Cathedral of the Holy Cross. Located in Boston's South End neighborhood, the cathedral was completed in 1875 and since that time has been the home of Boston's archbishops. It is often considered the spiritual center of Catholic Boston. (Courtesy of the archive of the Archdiocese of Boston.)

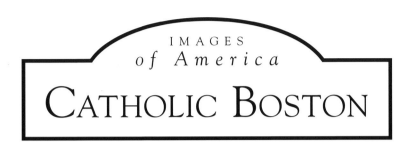

IMAGES
of America

CATHOLIC BOSTON

Thomas P. Lester
Foreword by Card. Seán O'Malley, OFM Cap

ARCADIA
PUBLISHING

Published by Arcadia Publishing
Charleston, South Carolina

Printed in the United States of America

Library of Congress Control Number: 2018932368

For all general information, please contact Arcadia Publishing:
Telephone 843-853-2070
Fax 843-853-0044
E-mail sales@arcadiapublishing.com
For customer service and orders:
Toll-Free 1-888-313-2665

Visit us on the Internet at www.arcadiapublishing.com

For my parents, Steven and Gladys

CONTENTS

FOREWORD

The coming pages feature photographs depicting the Catholic community of Boston and the people, places, and events that comprise our rich history.

The earliest members of our Catholic community arrived in Boston from Europe, largely France and Ireland, and many times coming via Canada, during the late 18th and early 19th centuries. These early arrivals trickled into the area slowly, often facing ridicule and persecution. Over the course of the ensuing decades, they would be joined by many more Catholics from a variety of countries and cultures around the world, but all of whom drew upon their faith as their source of strength. Arriving on new shores, their fellow Catholics were waiting with open arms to help them settle in their new home, more often than not displaying the virtues we strive for.

For those Bostonians who do not identify as Catholic, we share a common history as well. It is a story that illustrates how we have come to better understand one another and work together to make our community a better place. In the end, we all call Boston our home.

I hope everyone who has a connection with the Boston area and the Catholic community that resides there can find some joy in the history and memories depicted in this work.

I wish to acknowledge the outstanding work of Thomas P. Lester, archivist and records manager of the Archdiocese of Boston. He captures the great diversity of our people and the important role the Catholic Church has played in Greater Boston for over 200 years.

God bless,
Card. Seán P. O'Malley, Order of Friars Minor Capuchin
Archbishop of Boston

ACKNOWLEDGMENTS

I am very grateful for all of the help I received to make this book a reality. First and foremost, I want to thank my wife, Alexandra, whose continued encouragement and support was unrelenting throughout the process.

I also wish to acknowledge the contributions of MaryJo Donzella, archivist at the Archdiocese of Boston, who helped search the archive and *The Pilot* collections for photographs and scanned many of the images in the upcoming pages.

I would also like to thank the institutions that contributed images to this work, including the Boston Athenaeum, Boston College, College of the Holy Cross (Worcester, Massachusetts), Massachusetts State Archive (Boston), Museum of Fine Arts (Boston), St. Mary's Center for Women and Children (Boston), West End Museum (Boston), and the Knights of Columbus Museum (New Haven, Connecticut). Deserving of special mention are the staff of *The Pilot*, America's oldest Catholic newspaper and the official newspaper of the Archdiocese of Boston, who allowed me access to their photograph archive from which many of the upcoming images originate.

And, finally, thanks go to my colleagues at the Archdiocese of Boston for their assistance proofreading, fact-checking, and most of all for their encouragement over the past months. And a special thank-you is given to Card. Seán P. O'Malley, Order of Friars Minor Capuchin, archbishop of Boston, for his support of this project and for the kind words conveyed in the foreword.

Unless otherwise noted, all images appear courtesy of the archive of the Archdiocese of Boston.

INTRODUCTION

Catholicism made an inauspicious start in Boston, making its rise to prominence in the community during the 20th century so much more remarkable. Puritan roots ran deep in New England, and it was illegal to practice Catholicism in Massachusetts until 1780, and even then, scarcely tolerated. The first public Mass was not celebrated until eight years later.

From persecution and obscurity, the community sprang to life out of seemingly nothing. The foundations of the Catholic Church in the city are often attributed to two French priests, Fr. Francis Anthony Matignon and Fr. Jean Cheverus, who arrived in 1792 and 1796, respectively. They healed the Catholic community, which had been fractured by their loyalty to one of the two priests stationed there. Through their tireless and selfless work, they slowly earned the respect of both Catholic and non-Catholics alike, bringing these groups closer together.

Fathers Matignon and Cheverus faced a seemingly insurmountable task. Based in Boston, they were responsible for the care of Catholics throughout New England, traveling by horse, boat, and foot to tend to their flock. One major milestone during this era was the construction of the first Catholic church in New England, the Church of the Holy Cross, completed in 1803. A sign of the growing respect for the work of these two individuals is evident in the register of contributors toward its construction, among them a former president of the United States, John Adams.

By 1808, the Catholic community had developed enough to justify Pope Pius VII establishing the Diocese of Boston, whose borders then encompassed all of New England. Father Cheverus was named the diocese's first bishop, and under his watch, the community continued to grow. Assistance came with the arrival of priests from abroad, and he did also ordain Fr. Dennis Ryan, the first priest to be ordained in the city. Recalled to his native France in 1823, Bishop Cheverus left his adopted home with a heavy heart, a sentiment shared among all Bostonians as he departed.

It was uncertain whether Bishop Cheverus would return, and for two years, the status quo was maintained in anticipation of news. Then, in November 1825, Bishop Benedict Joseph Fenwick arrived to announce himself as the second bishop of Boston and thus began what is referred to as the "second founding" of the diocese. Bishop Fenwick began to build a formal structure and institutions to help support the growing Catholic community. From previous experience, as a young priest in the Diocese of New York, it was ingrained in him that to be successful and grow dioceses needed a college for boys, a convent school for girls, and an orphan asylum; he would succeed at establishing all three.

He invited the Sisters of Charity of Emmitsburg, Maryland, to join him in Boston, and within a few years, they opened St. Vincent's Orphan Asylum for girls. He would also help the Ursuline Nuns relocate from Boston to neighboring Charlestown, which, at the time, was an independent city. There, they opened a convent school for girls, but in one of the most infamous nights in local Catholic history, it was burned to the ground by an anti-Catholic mob and was never to be rebuilt. The final piece of his plan was perhaps the most challenging, a college for boys; he eventually succeeded with the founding of the College of the Holy Cross in Worcester, which he hoped would educate young men who would later become priests and serve Catholics in the Boston area.

When Bishop Fenwick died, he was succeeded by Bishop John Bernard Fitzpatrick, the first Bostonian to serve as bishop of Boston, whose education and career had been carefully watched and supported by his predecessor. He would go to great lengths to help the thousands of Irish Catholic immigrants who arrived on Boston's shores during his tenure. These new arrivals were incredibly devout and desired churches in the neighborhoods where they settled, so to remedy the lack of local churches, they often supported construction costs with their own meager earnings, which spurred a period of growth. While Catholic education would not truly blossom until the early 20th century, it is worth noting that through the efforts of Jesuit priests, Boston College was established in 1864. This era also saw Boston Catholics, with much regret, leave the old Cathedral of the Holy Cross on Franklin Street. They celebrated Mass at a number of temporary sites around the city until a new cathedral could be completed, which would take longer than expected.

It would be Bishop Fitzpatrick's successor, Bishop John Joseph Williams, who would see through the completion of a new cathedral for Boston's Catholics. With the Civil War over, so too were many of the issues that caused the delay, primarily that funding and labor were not available. With those problems in the past, he worked with famed church architect Patrick C. Keely to draw the plans and saw the new cathedral completed between the years 1866 and 1875. Boston Catholics could once again be proud of what one might consider their spiritual home. To commemorate the Franklin Street cathedral, the old altar was moved to the basement crypt, where Bishops Fitzpatrick and Williams are buried. The expansive territory encompassed by the Diocese of Boston had been broken up, and new, smaller dioceses were created. With this, the Diocese of Boston became an archdiocese, and Bishop Williams was elevated to the first archbishop of Boston.

The next archbishop of Boston was Card. William Henry O'Connell, a native of Lowell, Massachusetts. His size was imposing and matched his personality. Socializing with some of the most influential people in society, he never backed away from the spotlight and was proudly traditional and Roman in his views. To some of his contemporaries, Boston Catholics in particular, this was a sign that their time had arrived, and he was a symbol of all they could become. However, to others, his traditional views, fondness for the spotlight, and lifestyle were offensive and distasteful. In addition, his disciplined facade was betrayed by several private scandals, like poor management of church finances, which he was known to treat as his own. Despite this, the Catholic community as a whole was evolving and beginning to take on a new role. They were seen less as outsiders and more as an integral part of the community, with members being elected to leadership positions in unprecedented numbers.

Card. Richard James Cushing was the next leader of Boston's Catholics. Raised in South Boston and educated in the city's public schools, he attended Boston College High School, Boston College, and later, St. John Seminary. He was ordained at the Cathedral of the Holy Cross. He finely balanced his role as archbishop of Boston, a position of increasing importance as the number of Catholics grew. He could be seen with politicians and celebrities and was recognizable in his own right. Contrary to his predecessor, he was humble in his demeanor and shared a connection with his flock through their common upbringing, accent, and faith.

While an overview of these men, their character, and their contributions might provide a valuable way to assess the history of Catholic Boston, we cannot forget its people. It is they who have made Catholic life in Boston, as well as the surrounding cities and towns, so vibrant, welcoming, and enduring for over 200 years.

Even before the founding of St. Vincent's Orphan Asylum in 1843, the Catholics poured their hearts, money, and ideas into institutions of charity. Orphan asylums, industrial schools, and other institutions gave children a place to live, an education, skills, and the opportunity for a fulfilling life. Catholic hospitals treated patients, some turned away from other hospitals, often at no charge. Funds were raised for the poor Irish suffering from famine and, later, for those who had suffered through two horrible wars in Europe.

Similar efforts were put forth to develop Catholic education. Though early successes were made through the establishment of the College of the Holy Cross and Boston College during the 19th century, other educational institutions were much slower to evolve. By the early 20th century, a parish was not considered complete until it had a grammar school of its own. There were other notable achievements, such as the Sisters of Notre Dame de Namur, who already operated several Catholic schools in the city and who established Emmanuel College, the first Catholic girls' college in New England, in 1919.

Organizations for laypeople were an integral part of Catholic life in 20th-century Boston. Many evolved around the professions of those involved, forming guilds for health care, legal, and public safety professionals. Not only did they enrich their professional lives but also their spiritual lives, offering their professional services to others as an act of charity. Many had the aim of helping a particular group, such as the Guild for the Deaf or Guild for the Blind, with volunteers of the latter lending their time as readers and drivers.

Perhaps because of the scrutiny and persecution the earliest Catholics endured, they have always welcomed newcomers. With each successive wave of immigrants came new cultures, traditions, languages, and ideas that enriched the community as never before. And while such diversity existed at home, many Boston Catholics sought to share their faith abroad. Missionary work remained an important activity, and regular pilgrimages abroad enriched individuals' understanding of our faith.

Finally, within this larger Boston Catholic community reside many parishes. Here, friends and neighbors meet to worship together. It is in these close-knit groups that people socialize and support each other on a daily basis. Their fellow parishioners are like family, and church is as familiar as home. The smell of incense, the pastor's voice, and the light shining through the stained-glass windows comfort those who share a common faith.

This book traces the evolution of the Catholic Church in the Greater Boston area from its humble beginnings in the 18th century through the death of Card. Richard J. Cushing, archbishop of Boston, in 1970. I hope you enjoy connecting with the people, places, and events portrayed in the coming pages.

One

A Brief History of Catholicism in Boston

This July 14, 1898, photograph shows Tremont Street in Boston. In the distance rises the spire of Holy Trinity Catholic Church, located on Shawmut Avenue. Today, as in 1898, Boston is synonymous with the Catholic community that resides there. Strange as it may seem, that was not always the case, as the earliest Catholics were outsiders in a region steeped in Puritan tradition. (Courtesy of *The Pilot*.)

The changing sentiments of 18th-century Bostonians toward Catholics are well represented by John Adams. Like many, he was suspicious of Catholics because of a perceived susceptibility to influence from Rome, but his opinion changed as the American Revolution took shape. He met Catholic patriots—and even attended a Catholic Mass—while in Philadelphia with the Continental Congress. There were also political considerations, as the British colonies courted both Canada and France as potential allies. Exposure and necessity had changed his views by the time he was elected as a delegate to the Massachusetts Constitutional Convention, which met on September 1, 1779. Adams would be the primary author of the Declaration of Rights, and Article II of the document offered freedom to worship any religion a citizen chose, assuming it did not disturb the public peace or inhibit another from doing so. (Courtesy of the Massachusetts State Archive, Boston.)

Originally holding services in private homes, the Abbé Claude de la Poterie presided at the first public Catholic Mass on November 2, 1788. The abbé, whose real name was Claude Florent Bouchard, arrived with a French fleet that anchored in Boston Harbor from August 28 to September 28, 1788, remaining in the city after its departure. The Mass was held in a former Huguenot chapel (the building on the left with the archways), most recently used by Congregationalists, located at 18 School Street, across from the former city hall. In a moment that would resonate throughout time, the abbé exposed a piece of the True Cross for veneration, thus giving that church, and all future iterations, including today's cathedral, the name Holy Cross. Today, a plaque on the building marks the occasion. (Courtesy of the Knights of Columbus Museum, New Haven, Connecticut.)

The Diocese of Baltimore was created on November 6, 1789, and Fr. John Carroll (pictured) was appointed its first bishop. The diocese's boundaries matched those of the new United States, whose first president, George Washington, was inaugurated in April of the same year. With such a vast geographic area to oversee, Bishop Carroll urged Rome to create additional dioceses to better serve the Catholics living there.

Bishop Carroll sent Fr. Francis Matignon to serve the Catholics in Boston who were split over their loyalty to two priests there. He arrived on August 20, 1792, and immediately repaired the fractured community. Over time, he improved relations with the non-Catholic community, oversaw construction of the first Catholic church in New England, and invited a fellow Frenchman, Fr. Jean Cheverus, to help him serve Catholics in that region.

Fr. Jean Cheverus arrived in Boston on October 3, 1796. Contemporaries commented on his pious nature, captivating speaking skills, and energy with which he went about his work. When the Diocese of Boston was created in 1808, he became its first bishop. This portrait, by American painter Gilbert Stuart, was commissioned in 1823, shortly before Bishop Cheverus returned to his native France. (Courtesy of the Museum of Fine Arts, Boston.)

CATHEDRAL OF THE HOLY CROSS.
FRANKLIN ST. BOSTON.
DEDICATED SEPT. 29TH 1803.
Length 115 feet greatest width 72 feet.

In the autumn of 1799, Father Matignon purchased land on Franklin Street, Boston. The purchase, and his intention to build a new church for Boston's burgeoning Catholic population, was announced on Christmas Day of that year. Charles Bullfinch, who had designed the recently completed Massachusetts State House and would later work on the US Capitol, was contracted to design it.

It was with great sadness that Bostonians learned of Father Matignon's death on September 15, 1818. After a funeral Mass at the Franklin Street cathedral, he was temporarily laid to rest at the Granary Burying Ground, but Bishop Cheverus desired a more befitting resting place for his dear friend and colleague. In November 1818, the city approved his request to purchase land for a Catholic cemetery, which he did the following month. Father Matignon's body was reinterred at the new location, St. Augustine Cemetery, and the following year a chapel was constructed over the spot where he lay, dedicated on July 4, 1819. At various points in time, Mass was regularly celebrated at the chapel until 1871, when the nearby St. Augustine Church was completed. Above, the chapel stands among the gravestones in the cemetery, and at right, markers in the floor indicate those who have been buried underneath the chapel. The chapel is still in use today. (Both, courtesy of *The Pilot*.)

In 1823, Bishop Cheverus departed Boston for his native France and served as bishop of Montauban in 1824 and archbishop of Bordeaux in 1826. A decade later, he was named a cardinal but died on July 19, 1836, at the age of 68, before being ordained as such. This print, produced in Paris the same year, shows a much older Cardinal Cheverus in vestments reflecting his new status.

Following Bishop Cheverus's departure, it was unknown whether he would return until November 30, 1825, when his successor, Bishop Benedict Joseph Fenwick, arrived in Boston. He is described as being nearly six feet tall and having a large frame, dark complexion, and thick curly hair with an honest appearance. An extrovert, Bishop Fenwich was known for his wit.

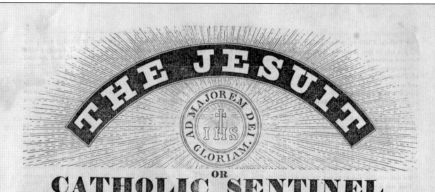

THE JESUIT

AD MAJOREM DEI GLORIAM. IHS

CATHOLIC OR SENTINEL.

Εἰ ὁ Θεὸς ὑπὲρ ἡμῶν, τίς καθ' ἡμῶν ;—SI DEUS PRO NOBIS, QUIS CONTRA NOS !—IF GOD BE FOR US, WHO IS AGAINST US !—ROM. VIII. XXXI.

VOL. I.   **BOSTON, SATURDAY, SEPTEMBER 5, 1829.**   **NO. I.**

The JESUIT, Published weekly, (to appear every Saturday,) by S. CONDON & F. S. EATON, for the PROPRIETORS, at $3 per annum, in advance.—All Communications must be post paid, and directed to the Editors of the "JESUIT," Boston, Mass.

The object is to explain, diffuse and defend the Principles of the ONE, HOLY, CATHOLIC and APOSTOLIC CHURCH.

. OFFICE......No. 14, State-Street.

PROSPECTUS.

The rapid increase and respectability of the Roman Catholics in Boston and through-out the New-England States, loudly call for the publication of a Newspaper, in which the Doctrine of the Holy Catholic Church, ever the same, from the Apostolic Age down to our time, may be truly explained, and moderately, but firmly defended.

We are fully aware of the crying calumnies, and gross misrepresentations which in this section of our country have been so long, so unsparingly, so cruelly heaped upon that Church, which alone influenced and directed the world for Sixteen Centuries ; which still, with the exception of a few, sectarian Countries, governs it, and which, unclouded as it ever has been by human passion, unmoved by individual caprice, will continue to shed its pure and hallowed light around the nations of the earth, until Time grows dim, and nature sinks into universal night.

A certain body of men, styling themselves Teachers in Israel, have shamefully abused the credulity and generous confidence of their respective Congregations, of the country at large. They went about, not doing good, but disseminating falsehoods and working evil. All this they unblushingly accomplished, under the mask of Religion ; in their Tracts,

at their Meetings, from their Pulpits !!! The Catholic, however meritorious, was branded with infamy, was ridiculed as ignorant, was viewed with abhorrence, was considered as a moral monster, as abominable and idolatrous !!! Much as the times are altered for the better, we deeply regret that even at the present day the various Sectarian Presses groan under the oppressive, indecorous calumnies of virulence and abuse. Conscience and Religion imperiously call upon us to check, as far as we can, this abomination of desolation, and to purge "the ear of Denmark" of the rank abuse by which it is diseased. Our anticipated labours are much relieved by the pleasing consideration that, the good sense of the community, added to the practical conviction, even here, of the salutary effects of that Religion, which flourishes amidst opposition, will lead them, from a free spirit of inquiry, so characteristic of them, in defiance to the loud denunciations of their Teachers, to see, read and judge for themselves. We venture to predict that, many will be found to say with Gamaliel of old, " Now therefore, I say to you, refrain from these men, and let them alone: for if this design, or work, be of men, it will fall to nothing. But if it be of God, you are not able to destroy it ; lest perhaps you be found to oppose God. And they consented to him." May God soften their hearts to do likewise ! The innate love of justice, and the discernment of the New-Englanders will not, cannot be much longer duped by a Pharisnical conspiracy ; the object of which seems to be, to impose, on the minds of freemen, fetters of the most galling, degrading character. Religious Truth has, thanks to Heaven, at last burst its

way through the misty atmosphere of Prejudice ; is triumphantly scattering the dark and noxious clouds from the region of the mind, and boldly rolls on in all the vigour of successful enterprise, in its congenial sphere of Freedom. To impart fresh impetus to its pervading power, it has been thought advisable to start a Publication which may aid it in its course.

We seek not battle, yet shall never shrink from it when forced upon us. Our banner is "Glory to God on high, and on earth peace to men of good will." Should the enemy assail us in our camp, or on our march, we shall invariably observe an honourable mode of warfare.—We scorn to break a lance with the scurrilous and vulgar combatant.

We have taken up our Cross, and doubt not, under Divine Providence, that a success similar to that which led a Constantine to victory awaits us. Should the trumpet sound to battle, we also are ready. In God is our trust ; under him, we as Sentinel and Soldier shall " fight the good fight ;" the scales of triumph and defeat are in His hands—"His will be done on earth."

The Religion which we advocate never required human succour. Its adoption only demands a patient, unprejudiced investigation. This will be certainly allowed it by a liberal and intelligent Public, who might have been led astray by " the false doctrines of men," on whom the punishment of their abominations will be visited.

Should the income of this paper exceed its expenses, the overplus will be exclusively devoted to the establishment of a Roman Catholic Asylum in Boston, or its immediate vicinity, for the maintenance and education of

During a visit to Hartford, Connecticut, Bishop Fenwick met with Francis Taylor, who founded a Catholic newspaper there titled the *Press*. Inspired, Bishop Fenwick returned to Boston determined to start a Catholic newspaper of his own and succeeded when *The Jesuit*, or *Catholic Sentinel*, appeared on September 5, 1829. The purpose of this weekly publication was to "explain, diffuse and defend the Principles of the ONE, HOLY, CATHOLIC, and APOSTOLIC CHURCH." It appeared under several titles in the ensuing two decades, including the *United States Catholic Intelligencer*, the *Literary and Catholic Sentinel*, the *Boston Pilot*, and *The Pilot*, the latter of which it has retained since 1858. The inaugural issue stated that any surplus profits would be directed toward "the establishment of a Roman Catholic Asylum in Boston, or its immediate vicinity, for the maintenance and education of poor Catholic children." While the orphanage would eventually come into existence, the newspaper never achieved the financial stability to support such an endeavor. (Courtesy of Boston College Theology and Ministry Library, Boston, Massachusetts.)

Struggling to retain readership and financial viability, Bishop Fenwick sold his newspaper to Patrick Donahoe (pictured) and his partner, Henry L. Devereux, in 1834. Donahoe was born in Munnery, County Cavan, Ireland, on March 17, 1811. He immigrated to Boston at the age of 10 and, several years later, began work in the printing industry. Scarcely two years after its purchase, the fate of *The Pilot* was endangered when Devereux left to start another publication. The circumstances forced Donahoe to cease operations for several months, but he resumed in 1838 under the moniker *Boston Pilot*, after the pro-Catholic *Dublin Pilot*. Under Donahoe, the newspaper's readership soared, largely due to the incorporation of the latest news from Ireland and Europe in addition to its theological content. Remarkably, he continued to serve as editor until his death in 1901. (Courtesy of *The Pilot*.)

James Augustine Healy (left) and Alexander Sherwood Healy (below) were two of several children born to Michael Healy, an Irish immigrant, and his wife, Eliza Clark, a former slave. The family resided in Georgia, where social status was determined by one's mother, so Michael sent his children north to offer them better opportunities. James graduated first in the inaugural class at the College of the Holy Cross, Worcester, and would continue his studies at seminaries in Montreal and Paris. After returning to Boston, he was named the first chancellor of the diocese and, in 1875, became the bishop of Portland, Maine. Alexander Sherwood, called "Sherwood," was chaplain at the House of the Angel Guardian, supervised construction of the Cathedral of the Holy Cross in Boston's South End, and was pastor of St. James, Boston, until meeting an early death in 1875.

Tall, graceful, and dignified in appearance, Bishop John Bernard Fitzpatrick had an equally impressive mind. He was described as possessing an even temperament, sparkling wit, and sound judgement. His tenure as the leader of Catholic Boston would see an influx of Irish Catholic immigrants, whom he made a concerted effort to assist through acts of charity.

This 1859 photograph depicts the Franklin Street church. From the creation of the Diocese of Boston in 1808, it was referred to as the Cathedral of the Holy Cross and served as the spiritual home of Boston's Catholics. It was sold one year after this photograph was taken to help fund the construction of the current Cathedral of the Holy Cross in Boston's South End.

Bishop Fitzpatrick struggled with his health for a number of years before dying on February 12, 1866, at 53 years of age. His tenure as bishop coincided with one of the most significant periods of growth. In 1846, the year he became bishop of Boston, the diocese consisted of 38 churches, with five more under construction, and a Catholic population of 65,000. By 1866, there were 109 churches, with six under construction, and an estimated Catholic population of over 350,000. In his later years, he was often absent in an attempt to cure his various ailments, at which time Fr. John Joseph Williams filled in as administrator and was therefore an ideal candidate for his successor. He is pictured above in 1871, four years before the diocese would be elevated to archdiocese, making him the first archbishop of Boston.

This c. 1870 photograph shows the current cathedral under construction. Building the new cathedral was delayed by the outbreak of the Civil War. In 1866, Bishop Williams met with architect Patrick Keely to review plans from several years earlier, and ground was broken in 1867. The structure, completed in 1875, was built in an English Gothic style and was designed to rival the great cathedrals of Europe.

Patrick Keely, architect of the new cathedral, was born in Ireland and most likely learned his trade from his father before arriving in the United States in the early 1840s. In 1848, he completed his first church, SS. Peter and Paul, Brooklyn, and would continue to design 16 cathedrals and an estimated 500 to 700 churches in the United States and Canada during his lifetime. (Courtesy of *The Pilot*.)

The South End was chosen for the new cathedral because it was one of the most desirable areas in the city to live at the time. Unforeseen was the construction of the Boston Elevated Railway, which would run directly across the cathedral's front, altering the complexion of the neighborhood. Pictured here, Bostonians use it as a platform to view the deceased Cardinal O'Connell at his requiem Mass in April 1944.

Bishop William Henry O'Connell succeeded Archbishop Williams following the latter's death in 1907. He had a commanding physical appearance, always carrying himself erect to make the most of his five-foot, eight-inch frame and 250-plus pounds. He was not only an imposing figure physically but also lived in grand style and never shied away from the public eye, which was in stark contrast to the humble, modest, and rather secluded Archbishop Williams.

Pictured here are, from left to right, Msgr. Francis L. Phelan, chancellor of the Archdiocese of Boston; Cardinal O'Connell, archbishop of Boston; Card. Eugenio Pacelli, later Pope Pius XII; and Bishop Francis Spellman during a visit to St. John Seminary, Brighton, on October 13, 1936.

While it had previously weathered periods of financial instability, *The Pilot* found itself at risk once again, largely due to the appearance of newspapers in other dioceses and a decline in Irish immigration. In an effort to tie it once more to the Archdiocese of Boston and have an organ to announce its centennial celebration, Cardinal O'Connell purchased the publication on September 14, 1908. (Courtesy of *The Pilot*.)

Divided opinions aside, Boston Catholics found a strong leader in Cardinal O'Connell, who would guide them through two world wars. Here, in 1918, he presides at Mass with military personnel at Fort Devens, Massachusetts, which housed soldiers waiting for deployment. He would die shortly before the end of World War II.

In 1926, Cardinal O'Connell commissioned Boston architects McGinnis and Walsh to construct a new residence for himself in Brighton, near St. John Seminary. What resulted was a three-story home built in the Italian Renaissance style and finished in limestone. This was his fourth home, following the cathedral rectory, a home in Boston's Back Bay, and finally, one on Fisher Hill in Brookline—each residence seemingly more extravagant than the last.

On April 22, 1944, Card. William Henry O'Connell died. While he sometimes faced criticism for his elegant lifestyle and frequent absences while traveling abroad, his tenure also saw the Catholic community gain a strong foothold in the Boston area, and he capably lead the community through two world wars. Per his wishes, he was laid to rest on the grounds of St. John Seminary, Brighton.

With the death of Cardinal O'Connell came Bishop Richard Cushing, installed as archbishop of Boston at the Cathedral of the Holy Cross on November 8, 1944. Born in South Boston, he shared a special connection with Boston's Catholics, who would see their numbers and influence reach unprecedented heights during his tenure.

By this time, Boston Catholics no longer questioned their important role in the local community. Pictured here with Cardinal Cushing (right) is Boston mayor John F. Collins, another example of a local Irish Catholic who rose to prominence in the community. Collins was born in Roxbury, served two terms as mayor, and when he died in 1995, his funeral was held at the Cathedral of the Holy Cross.

Perhaps most symbolic of the community's rise was the popularity of Pres. John F. Kennedy. Joined by the rest of the nation, Bostonians mourned the loss of this rising star following his assassination, holding a memorial Mass at the Cathedral of the Holy Cross on January 19, 1964. Seated in the front, center, pew are members of President Kennedy's immediate family. Sitting on the far right of the pew is his widow, Jackie Kennedy.

A notable feature of the Cardinal Cushing era was the use of technology to reach Catholics residing in Boston and beyond. Midnight Mass on Christmas Eve 1949 was the first time a Catholic Mass was televised in the city of Boston. It took a crew of 17 people one week to prepare the sound and video equipment. Church officials were quick to point out that watching Mass on television was not a substitute for attending in person. Radio was also widely used, and in the undated photograph at right, Cardinal Cushing speaks into a microphone during a WCOP radio broadcast. Through these mediums Cardinal Cushing saw an opportunity to reach people throughout their everyday lives, not just at Mass on Sundays. His unrelenting construction of chapels and churches also helped make worship more accessible.

With Cardinal Cushing in failing health, his successor, Bishop Humberto Sousa Medeiros, was installed as the archbishop of Boston on October 7, 1970. The following month, on November 2, 1970, Cardinal Cushing died. They are pictured here, together, speaking to members of the press at the cardinal's residence in Brighton.

The Cathedral of the Holy Cross is pictured in the 1960s, a period when the Boston Catholic community was approaching its xenith in terms of numbers and influence. Cardinal Cushing's tenure saw the Catholic population within the Archdiocese of Boston grow from 1,155,201 in 1944 to 1,914,350 in 1970. This was matched by the construction of over 80 new churches and chapels, six hospitals, and the introduction of 60 new religious orders.

Two

SERVING THE COMMUNITY

This print of St. Vincent's Orphan Asylum, the first Catholic charitable institution in the city of Boston, dates to the year it was established, 1843. The building pictured here could house up to 500 orphaned girls, and though the institution would move to various locations, it would continue to serve for over 100 years, closing in 1949.

Sr. Ann Alexis Shorp, of the Daughters of Charity from Emmitsburg, Maryland, arrived with two companions on May 2, 1832, at the request of Bishop Fenwick. The sisters operated a day school for poor female students, cared for orphaned girls, and organized charity fairs to raise funds for an orphan asylum. In 1843, they opened St. Vincent's Orphan Asylum, whose enduring success was attributed to Sr. Ann Alexis, who was in charge of its daily operations from 1843 until her death in 1875. The institution moved several times throughout its history. Pictured below is the asylum at 52 Camden Street, where it relocated in 1929. This smaller site housed eight Daughters of Charity and two lay teachers who were responsible for the care of 87 girls.

The photograph above depicts a rather simply furnished classroom. The teacher at left, a member of the Daughters of Charity, instructs a class of charges residing at St. Vincent's Orphan Asylum. Pictured below, girls line up to take a turn on the slide, while a sister supervises them. Other girls are seen swinging in the background. Both of these photographs were taken in the 1940s, by which time the institution had moved to 45 Guyette Road, Cambridge. Sadly, its long history of service would cease at the end of the decade.

34

The Charitable Irish Society, founded in 1737, is the oldest Irish society in the Americas. Its earliest members were largely Protestant Irish, but it made no distinction, providing assistance to those who followed them across the Atlantic Ocean by finding suitable housing, employment, and other assistance as needed. The society also contributed to other causes, such as in 1794 when it provided Father Matignon with funds to purchase school books for poor Catholic children. In 1806, 1810, and each year since 1814, the archbishop of Boston has been invited to attend the society's annual St. Patrick's Day banquet. Pictured here, Archbishop O'Connell can be seen to the left, at the head table, at the 175th anniversary dinner of the society, held at the Somerset Hotel, Boston, on March 18, 1912. The Charitable Irish Society continues its mission even today.

The House of the Angel Guardian opened in Boston's North End on June 1, 1851, and helped homeless boys by giving them a place to live and finding them jobs or apprenticeships. Initially, the house was financially sustained by its founder, Fr. George Haskins, and also by some residents who worked and paid a small fee to board there. Some of the boys were there for temporary stays, if deemed unruly by their parents.

REV. GEO, F. HASKINS.

Father Haskins continued to run the institution until his death on October 5, 1872. Its operation was continued by the Brothers of Charity of Montreal, who built a trade school in 1887 to teach the boys practical skills. At times, the brothers had 300 boys in their care. They also moved the institution from the crowded North End to the Jamaica Plain neighborhood. Pictured below is the House of the Angel Guardian band from 1924.

The Home for Destitute Catholic Children originated with a charity school founded by Protestant Samuel Eliot in 1850. The Diocese of Boston is believed to have had some role in its administration by 1856, and in 1864, the Association for the Protection of Destitute Catholic Children formed and assumed responsibility for the institution, changing its name in the process. Much of the support for Eliot's school continued to come from Protestant philanthropists as it evolved over time, including when the tireless Daughters of Charity of Emmitsburg replaced the lay staff in 1866. The institution served as a temporary home for children before being returned to their parents or placed with a new family. It was later renamed Nazareth. Above, standing outside of Nazareth, Cardinal Cushing is pictured with residents and administrators in 1959. Below is an aerial view of the campus.

ANDREW CARNEY

A major contributor to many Catholic charities was Andrew Carney, born May 12, 1794, in Ballanagh, County Cavan, Ireland. He arrived in Boston in 1816 and, after saving enough of his earnings, opened a tailor shop in 1830. He was one of the first tailors in the area to offer ready-made clothing, which earned him contracts making uniforms for the Army, and by 1845, he was able to retire, by all accounts, the wealthiest Catholic in New England. He is described as being warmhearted, openhanded, honorable, and pious. He would spend the remainder of his life managing his wealth and focusing on philanthropy, contributing his time and money to good causes such as St. Vincent's Orphan Asylum, Boston College, the Sisters of St. Vincent de Paul, Clergy Fund Society, the new Cathedral of the Holy Cross, and many others. (Courtesy of *The Pilot*.)

Another project that achieved success with the support of Andrew Carney was the hospital that still bears his name. He purchased an estate for such a purpose in 1863, pictured above, and provided an endowment for its long-term support. When the institution opened its doors in July of that year, the entire staff consisted of two sisters and two laymen in the charge of Sr. Ann Alexis. This was the first institution of its kind in Boston, offering affordable health care to those who would otherwise be unable to afford it or were refused treatment elsewhere. For a time, starting in 1868, it also included an infant asylum to care for unwed mothers, a forerunner of St. Mary's Infant Asylum later established in Dorchester. Pictured below are hospital staff members working at the original site in the 1860s. (Both, courtesy of *The Pilot*.)

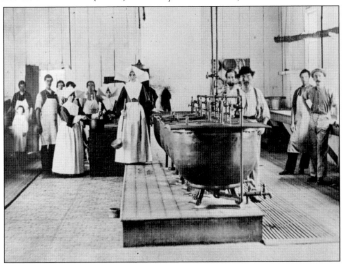

Carney Hospital has moved several times during its existence. The original site was not ideal, having originally been a private home, and also carried a large debt. In 1882, the institution moved to the corner of Cushing and Everett Avenues in Dorchester. At its new location, the Sisters of Charity of Nazareth were briefly put in charge, followed by the Daughters of Charity of Emmitsburg in 1893. The latter helped it reach financial stability and expanded the operation. This overhead view from 1978 shows the hospital at its current location in Dorchester, which opened in 1953. (Both, courtesy of *The Pilot*.)

In 1868, the Sisters of the Third Order of St. Francis opened St. Elizabeth Hospital. The hospital admitted only women until 1882. It was renowned for its gynecology department and the free-of-charge care it offered to the poor. From 1880 to 1896, it operated a second location in Roxbury, and in 1896, an outpatient department was added to the original hospital, which is pictured here. (Courtesy of *The Pilot*.)

Needing to expand, land was purchased in Boston's Brighton neighborhood for a new hospital between 1910 and 1911, and ground was broken at the new site the following year. The hospital reopened at this new location on September 1, 1914, and included a chapel, convent, and nurses' home on the property. (Courtesy of *The Pilot*.)

Several attempts had been made to care for infants in need, including at the Home for Destitute Catholic Children and Carney Hospital, but it was eventually concluded that a more adequate facility was needed to care for babies and provide assistance to unwed mothers. To accomplish this, St. Mary's Infant Asylum and Lying-in Hospital was founded in 1874 and would become recognized for its then modern approach to sanitation, meals for patients, and treatment of childhood diseases. (Both, courtesy of St. Mary's Center for Women and Children, Boston.)

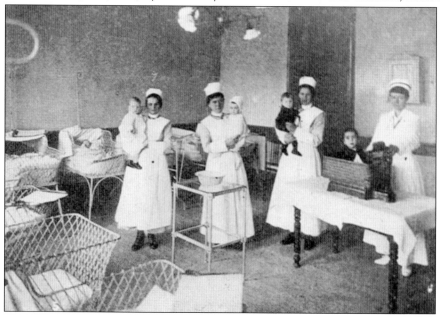

St. Margaret's Hospital for Women opened in Boston's Dorchester neighborhood on May 7, 1911, as an adjunct to St. Mary's Infant Asylum. Operated by the Daughters of Charity of St. Vincent de Paul, it was a gift of two local priests, Fr. Peter Ronan and his brother Fr. Michael Ronan, who named the hospital in honor of their mother. In 1929, it expanded into a general hospital to meet the demand for its services and established a school for nurses. Pictured at right is the hospital. Below, graduates from the nursing school receive their diplomas from Msgr. Augustine E. Dalton at St. Kevin, Dorchester. (Both, courtesy of *The Pilot*.)

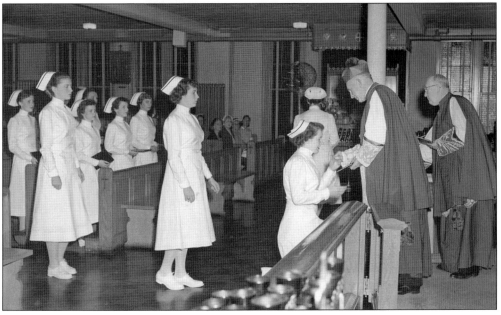

At left, Cardinal Cushing stands with three children, watching the foundation being dug for the Joseph P. Kennedy, Jr. Memorial Hospital, located on Warren Street in Boston's Brighton neighborhood. The hospital opened on September 8, 1949, and provided care for children with mental and physical disabilities. In addition to research, it was a place where children could convalesce following surgeries and overcome handicaps through rehabilitation. Below, Cardinal Cushing sits in a cart with several patients, while Henry R. Silver, treasurer and director of the Cott Bottling Company, who sponsored this party for the children, guides the donkey. (Both, courtesy of *The Pilot*.)

Care at the Kennedy Memorial Hospital was not limited to Catholic children and accepted any patient who required care. The hospital was staffed by the Franciscan Medical Missionaries of Mary, pictured above with Cardinal Cushing and several patients, and thus the name was later changed to the Franciscan Children's Hospital, which it still bears today. Below, patients receive a visit from Boston Celtics players, from left to right, Ed McCauley, Bob Brannum, Bob Cousy, Bill Sharman, and Don Barksdale in March 1955. To their right stands Hon. Thomas J. Spring, deputy of the Massachusetts Knights of Columbus. (Both, courtesy of *The Pilot*.)

On January 1, 1903, the Central Bureau of Information, the earliest iteration of what would become the Catholic Charitable Bureau, now Catholic Charities, opened. It monitored the well-being of Catholic orphans in institutions and those newly placed in homes. The organization also kept lists of suitable Catholic homes for those who were not yet placed. Pictured is Fr. Joseph G. Anderson, the Central Bureau of Information's first director. He would later become an auxiliary bishop of Boston.

During and after World War II, Boston's Catholics contributed generously to the relief of war-ravaged Europe. Organizations such as the War Relief Services and National Catholic Welfare Conference, the latter part of Catholic Charities, sent much-needed food, clothing, and other necessities abroad. This 1947 photograph shows supply trucks being unloaded.

Three

CATHOLIC EDUCATION

Students from St. Margaret's School in Boston's Dorchester neighborhood create a scene commemorating the work of St. Elizabeth Ann Seton, founder of the Sisters of Charity of St. Joseph, Emmitsburg, Maryland, who first arrived in Boston in 1832. She was a proponent of Catholic education, starting St. Joseph Academy and Free School in Emmitsburg, which is the scene recreated here. She was canonized on September 14, 1975.

Destruction of the Ursuline Convent by Fire.

The Ursuline Nuns arrived in Boston at the invitation of Bishop Cheverus in 1820. He built a convent and school for them next to the cathedral where they taught about 100 students, mostly poor Irish girls who paid no tuition. After a tuberculosis outbreak at the school, Madame St. George (née Mary Anne Moffatt) and Bishop Fenwick looked for a location outside of Boston that would be healthier for the sisters and their students and purchased land in Charlestown in 1826. The school, named Mount Benedict, is recognized as the first formal Catholic school in Boston. It was starkly different from its predecessor, charging tuition and largely serving the daughters of upper-class Unitarian families. On August 11, 1834, anti-Catholic rioters burned the site to the ground. It was never rebuilt.

Ruins of the Ursuline Convent on Mount Benedict.

In 1834, Bishop Fenwick purchased land in Aroostook County, Maine, and hoped to create a Catholic utopia. He thought the property, named Benedicta in his honor, would appeal to the poor Irish Catholics living in Boston, offering them a chance to work their own land, but the town failed to attract settlers. Undeterred, Bishop Fenwick tried to save it by establishing a seminary there, but the location was so remote that no religious order was willing to staff it. In 1843, he purchased Mount St. James Academy (right) in Worcester, Massachusetts, from Fr. James Fitton (below), who founded it in 1836. Following the purchase of the school, Bishop Fenwick took little further interest in Benedicta, which was incorporated by the State of Maine in 1871. (Both, courtesy of the College of the Holy Cross Photograph Archives, Worcester, Massachusetts.)

Catholic College of the Holy (

With the purchase of Mount St. James Academy, Bishop Fenwick was finally able to realize his dream of founding a school where aspiring priests could be educated and then go on to serve Boston and the surrounding area. He immediately set about making improvements, expanding the property from 52 to 84 acres and constructing a new four-story brick school building, which was completed in January 1844. In the intervening time, after some negotiation, he convinced

s, Worcester, Massachusetts.

the Society of Jesus (SJ) to staff the college, and classes commenced on November 1, 1843. In its first year, the school consisted of six faculty members and 12 students, but within three years, it grew to nine faculty members and nearly 100 students from various parts of the United States and Canada. Pictured here is a sketch of the college from an advertisement dating to 1881. (Courtesy of the College of the Holy Cross Photograph Archives, Worcester, Massachusetts.)

Fr. John McElroy, SJ (left), was pastor of St. Mary, Boston, from 1847 to 1863 and shared Bishop Fitzpatrick's desire to establish a Catholic college in Boston. After several failed attempts, he purchased three acres of land on Harrison Avenue in 1857, but projects to improve the land, financial hardships, and the Civil War all caused delays. Sadly, he would leave Boston in 1863 before the project was completed, but work would be continued by his successor Fr. John Bapst, SJ (below). With the assistance of Catholic philanthropist Andrew Carney, Boston College opened its doors on September 5, 1864. It was a day school, and tuition was kept low so as to provide an opportunity for boys of modest means to attend. Father Bapst served as its first president.

This stereo card contains images captured by Oliver Wendell Holmes. The building at left is the Immaculate Conception Church. The building at right is the original Boston College, in Boston's South End, where it stood until moving to the Chestnut Hill area in 1913. When viewed through a stereoscope, the two images on a stereo card would provide the viewer with a three-dimensional image.

Rising high above the Chestnut Hill Reservoir, Gasson Hall was the first building completed on Boston College's new Chestnut Hill campus. The building's namesake, Fr. Thomas I. Gasson, SJ, was the college's president at the time. He oversaw completion of the building, which opened in the spring of 1913, and moved the entire college out of Boston's South End in time for the new school year the following autumn. (Courtesy of the Boston College Burns Library.)

Above, Cardinal Cushing delivers an address at the 100th Boston College convocation in 1963. He shares the stage with several other dignitaries, including, from left to right, (first row) Dr. Nathan Marsh Pusey, president of Harvard College; Michael J. Walsh, SJ, president of Boston College; and Pres. John F. Kennedy. Behind them stands, from left to right, Edward Boland (glasses) and Thomas P. O'Neill, both representatives for the State of Massachusetts at the time.

Cardinal O'Connell poses with L. Lawrence Lowell, president of Harvard University, while there to receive an honorary degree in 1937. Boston Catholics equated Cardinal O'Connell's status as a symbol of their arrival to the mainstream, a situation the cardinal embellished to the fullest.

Cardinal Cushing poses with three graduates from the Academy of Notre Dame, Roxbury. The Sisters of Notre Dame de Namur were one of the first religious orders to arrive in Boston, in November 1849, at the invitation of Fr. John McElroy, SJ. The three sisters arrived from Cincinnati, and on November 15, they opened St. Mary Parochial School in the North End, instructing over 100 students in a small two-room school.

The sisters' achievements would continue for over 100 years, including founding Notre Dame Academy, which had schools in several locations. Their former Berkeley Street site was sold to the Knights of Columbus as the "Liberty House," and eventually, the academy settled in Roxbury. The sisters established and continued to operate many other institutions of learning, including Julie Billiart High School, whose students are pictured here at the Cathedral of the Holy Cross.

The Sisters of Notre Dame de Namur also founded Emmanuel College, the first Catholic women's college in New England, in 1919. Above, in 1955, Cardinal Cushing lunches with student leaders responsible for the building fund campaign to construct Marian Hall. From left to right sit Mary Kelley, Loeman Hayden, Alice Fellows, Cardinal Cushing, Rosemary Donahue, Rosemary LaMonica, and Jane Carolan. Throughout the first few decades, it was a commuter school, but expansions in the 1950s and 1960s offered students the opportunity to live on campus. The college remained a women's college until becoming coeducational in 2001. (Both, courtesy of *The Pilot*.)

Though Bishop Fenwick had established Holy Cross College, Worcester, it was realized that the school could not act as both college and seminary. For many years, a seminary in Boston had been discussed, and with the debt from the new cathedral repaid in 1879, Archbishop Williams was able to purchase a 26-acre estate in Brighton on March 22 of the following year.

Construction of the Theology House, pictured here in 1915, began on April 1881 and was completed three years later. Its edifice, made of pudding-stone quarried on site, is in the shape of an "L," which changed from the original plan for a full square to reduce the cost. The building was dedicated on September 18, 1884, and classes commenced for the first time on September 22.

St. John Seminary was one of Archbishop Williams's proudest achievements. The Philosophy House was dedicated October 23, 1890, and a new chapel was completed in 1899. Shown here, seminarians kneel in the aisle facing the chapel altar. Note the beautifully painted walls, completed by Gonippo Raggi, surrounding the altar.

When the seminary was constructed, the surrounding area was sparsely populated, but even as the area developed, there was ample room for seminarians to enjoy recreational activities around the grounds. Playing a game of ice hockey on Chandler Pond, seminarians take advantage of one of many cold New England winter days.

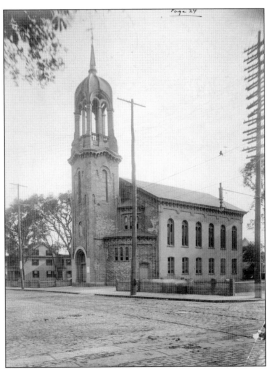

The photograph at right, taken on June 23, 1909, is of the Cheverus Centennial School. The school was attached to the parish of the Sacred Hearts of Jesus and Mary, in the Boston suburb of Malden. The parish was established in 1891 under the first pastor, Fr. Thomas H. Shahan. He hoped to open a school, but sadly, he died in 1902 at 81 years of age. His successor, Fr. Patrick Hally, worked toward the same end, eliminating the debt of building the parish's church and purchasing an old Universalist church at the corner of Main and Centre Streets for the parish school in 1908. Below, some of the students line up in the street to show their patriotism and salute the American flag.

The Cheverus Centennial School was named as such because the year it was established, 1908, was the 100th anniversary of Father Cheverus being named the first bishop of Boston. The Sisters of Providence of St. Mary-of-the-Woods staffed the school, and it opened on September 13, 1908, with 300 students in grades one through five. Pictured above and below are students in their classrooms on June 23, 1909. Sadly, six months later, the land was claimed for an elevated railway station, but luckily, a second site was purchased for a new school and convent for the sisters.

One of the more popular activities throughout the 20th century was seeing marching bands, drum and bugle corps, and other such organizations perform. Parishes would compete against one another in competitions, often organized by the Catholic Youth Organization; march in parades; and participate in other community events. Pictured here is a band from the Sacred Heart parish in Boston's Roslindale neighborhood.

In this undated photograph is the band from the Gate of Heaven Parish in South Boston. Before the parish had a school, classes for girls were held in the church basement as early as 1863 and, later, at St. Agnes School in South Boston. In 1922, the new Gate of Heaven School opened and admitted both boys and girls.

Shown here is the band of the Holy Name Parish, West Roxbury, in 1945. Displayed on the drum is the impressive record the band achieved of winning the best parochial school band in the Archdiocese of Boston for five years in a row. The school was established by the Sisters of St. Joseph and opened on September 10, 1953.

Pictured is a class from St. Margaret High School, located in Boston's Dorchester neighborhood. On September 14, 1910, the parish opened a grammar school and, later, a high school, which prepared students for college or normal school. In 1948, the high school was renamed Monsignor Ryan Memorial, after Msgr. William Ryan who served as pastor there for 54 years and died in 1947.

Four

CATHOLIC LAY ORGANIZATIONS

Pictured is a reception hosted by the Guild for the Blind; Fr. Thomas Carroll is seated at the back, center, of the table. In 1943, Cardinal O'Connell purchased an estate on Centre Street in Newton, a suburb of Boston, which became the Carroll Center for the Blind. When it opened, the main house, St. Raphael's Hall, contained 30 rooms intended for use by blind senior citizens and blind-deaf women.

At left, Cardinal Cushing and Fr. Thomas Carroll pose with confirmation candidates from the Guild for the Blind at St. Patrick Church, Watertown, on June 2, 1943. The guild served the blind of all faiths and formed from a series of retreats held as early as 1929 at the Cenacle Convent, St. Francis Friary, and Boston College. When the guild was formally organized, each retreat site became its own chapter, and two additional chapters were created to provide clothing for blind women and help the blind find employment. Sighted people were also recruited as readers, drivers, and volunteers in other capacities. Below, Cardinal Cushing speaks at the 10th anniversary of the guild.

Like the Guild for the Blind, there was also a Guild for the Deaf. Above, members gather for the inaugural meeting of the guild in 1949. Fr. John Watson, the first spiritual director of the group, stands in the back, center, of the picture; he is the shorter of the two priests. Pictured below, he is standing alongside Cardinal Cushing and a nurse. The piece of equipment shown was used to assess a patient's hearing. Note the hearing test diagnostic chart on the wall behind Cardinal Cushing. (Below, courtesy of *The Pilot*.)

David Goldstein and Martha Moore Avery met in the 1890s and converted to Catholicism in 1903 and 1905, respectively. Their ambition to reach Catholics on the street, at public meetings, and other such locales led them form the Catholic Truth Guild. Traveling in a van painted in papal colors, with the slogan "For God and Country" on the side, and flying an American Flag, they fulfilled their vision. Cardinal O'Connell blessed the van on July 1, 1917, and its first public event was the Fourth of July celebration on the Boston Common, which was attended by an estimated 5,000 people. Goldstein continued to tour the country for 20 years until old age prevented him from doing so. Depicted here, David Goldstein and Arthur Corbett, another guild member, sit in a car owned by the guild while it is blessed by Cardinal O'Connell.

Cardinal O'Connell stands with members of the St. Apollonia Guild in October 1940. On March 20, 1920, the guild was formed by 20 Catholic dentists from the Greater Boston area. Its primary philanthropic purpose was to provide affordable dental care to Catholic schoolchildren. The bus, donated by Joseph P. Kennedy, was used to transport 50 children at a time to the Forsyth Dental Infirmary where they were treated for a nominal fee of 25¢. Within a few months of the guild's formation, its numbers swelled from 20 to over 100 members, and in the coming years, the members treated tens of thousands of parochial school students. When it was not being used, the bus was lent to parishes and Catholic schools for outings.

Police officers depart the Cathedral of the Holy Cross, Boston, after a "Blue Mass" to celebrate public safety officials. Like the St. Apollonia Guild, other groups were established based on their members' professions, such as the St. Luke's Guild, which was formed by about 100 Catholic physicians and surgeons on May 14, 1910. Over the ensuing decades, the group would generally meet at Carney or St. Elizabeth's Hospitals to present papers on contemporary topics in medicine. Like the above celebration, a "White Mass" for medical professionals is held each year, and similarly, a "Red Mass" honors judges, lawyers, and other legal professionals.

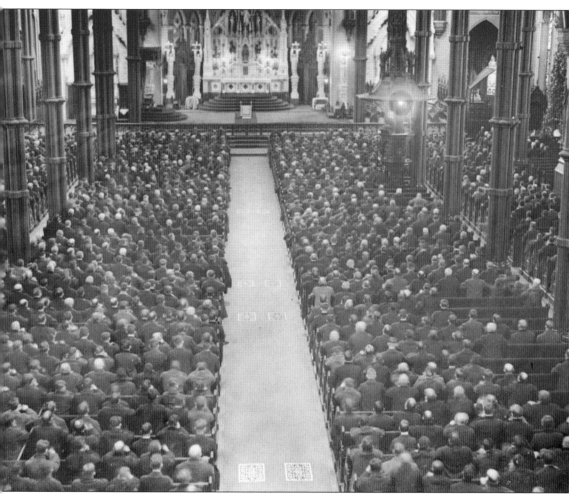

The Holy Name Society was omnipresent in the early and mid-20th century. Formed at the parish level, Cardinal O'Connell urged every parish to have a branch and for every man to join. Each year, on the Feast of the Holy Name, he would call on members from all the branches in the Archdiocese of Boston to assemble in the city to celebrate Mass at the Cathedral of the Holy Cross and renew their dedication to the society's mission, which "promotes reverence for the Sacred Names of God and Jesus Christ, obedience and loyalty to the Magisterium of the Catholic Church, and the personal sanctification and holiness of its members." Here, they are pictured filling the Cathedral of the Holy Cross, Boston, at one of these annual gatherings on January 4, 1920.

In 1924, Holy Name Society members from around the country gathered in the nation's capital to mark the 650th anniversary of the society, founded in 1274 as the Confraternity of the Most Holy Names of God and Jesus. Cardinal O'Connell was appointed papal legate to the Holy Name Society National Convention in Washington, DC, the first papal legate to be sent to a laymen's convention. Seated behind Cardinal O'Connell on his right is Archbishop Michael J. Curley, who served as the archbishop of Baltimore from 1921 to 1939 and of Baltimore and Washington, DC, from 1939 until his death in 1947. Below, members of the Sacred Heart, Mount Auburn (Watertown), Holy Name Society are in attendance at the national convention.

In 1947, it was Boston's turn to host a national convention for the Holy Name Society. Here, on October 3, 1947, members from around the country gather at Braves Field. To the left is a temporary sanctuary erected for the event, in front of which the last few members of the procession make their way down the center aisle to their seats. The photograph below, taken from the front left of the temporary sanctuary, shows those already seated in the stands looking on. At the time, the society was only open to laymen and clergy but has since changed, and women may now become members.

The Holy Name Society parading through the streets of Boston was not an uncommon sight in the 20th century. Above, participants from St. Kevin, Dorchester, are about to turn the corner of Charles and Boylston Streets during a parade on October 5, 1947. The advanced members carry a banner naming their parish, while behind march the remaining members, including a brass band and float. They trail behind a float from St. Ann Parish, Dorchester. Floats often depicted scenes from the Bible, saints, or other religious subjects. The photograph below is a close-up of St. Ann's float; St. Ann was the mother of the Blessed Virgin Mary.

Each parish's float was judged, and the best one was announced after the parade concluded. Above, the judges' stand, erected on Charles Street, offers shelter to a few local boys looking on. Below, the parade's marshal and his staff acknowledge Cardinal Cushing, Mayor John B. Hynes (of Boston), and Bishop John J. Wright, who stand on the viewing platform to the left. In 1908, the Archdiocese of Boston celebrated its centennial; that year, 40,000 Holy Name Society members marched in a parade that took five hours to pass the viewing stand.

Above, Archbishop Cushing walks among those attending a Holy Hour, organized by the Catholic Youth Organization at Boston College's Alumni Field, on September 19, 1945. The Catholic Youth Organization was formed seven years earlier to coordinate, support, and provided a balance of activities for Catholics between 10 and 26 years of age. Activities included scouting, sports teams, debates, and essay contests. A Holy Hour is an hour of prayer in veneration of Jesus's sufferings and was a popular event allowing Catholics to come together and share their faith with one another. Below, Cardinal Cushing stands at the temporary sanctuary leading the participants in prayer.

The first meeting of the League of Catholic Women, also known as the Catholic Women's Guild, is acknowledged to have taken place at the home of Elizabeth J. Dwight on Beacon Street, Boston, in 1910. They organized a meeting for those interested in joining the organization on May 2, 1910, at the Cathedral of the Holy Cross. Over 200 local Catholic women attended and were addressed by Cardinal O'Connell; Katherine E. Conway, former editor of *The Pilot*; and several others. Here, they gather at the Cathedral of the Holy Cross in the 1940s.

The league's mission was "to unite Catholic women for the promotion of religious, intellectual, and charitable work." It hosted lecture series and debates, maintained lists of volunteers and volunteer opportunities, visited the sick, read to the blind, and reclaimed lapsed Catholics. Its membership quickly rose to about 700 in number. All Catholic women of good standing were eligible to join, and annual dues were $1 each. Here, the league hosts a group of Girl Scouts during its annual meeting at the Statler Hilton Hotel, now the Park Plaza Hotel, which has been listed in the register of National Trust for Historic Preservation's list of Historic Hotels of America.

In addition to its regular charitable work, the Catholic Women's Guild had several special programs. With an influx of Italian immigrants arriving and settling in Boston's North End, members started a Sunday school for children, two sewing clubs for women, and hosted a number of other special activities to help them settle in their new country. The guild had a probation program that arranged for foster homes for young girls who had been sentenced in juvenile court and set up a "big sister" program to mentor them. This group also formed the nucleus of the Catholic Women's War Service Council in World War I, and during the Spanish flu epidemic of 1918, it set up aid stations with supplies and cared for the children of stricken parents. On stage, Fr. Francis J. Lally addresses the group.

Members of the Council of Catholic Women pose with Massachusetts governor John Volpe in the late 1960s. Volpe served two terms as governor (1960–1962 and 1964–1969). Pictured are, from left to right, Margaret O'Day, Catherine Egan, Governor Volpe, Margaret Vaccaso, Mary Fee, and Agnes Callahan.

Here, a Mass of the Archdiocesan Council of Catholic Women is being filmed in the chapel at the archbishop's residence in Brighton. Standing at the front of the aisle is Rev. Joseph P. Donelan, the group's chaplain, and to the back right, near the organ, is Msgr. Walter Flaherty, director of Boston Catholic Television.

This Ancient Order of Hibernian's building is in Boston's Roxbury neighborhood. The order was a group of Catholic laymen, formed in the mid-19th century, with the purpose of providing relief to members and their families and encouraging cooperation among the Irish in America. The founding members initially approached Bishop Fitzpatrick seeking his endorsement for such an organization in 1859, but there was a prevalent fear of secret societies, such as the Odd Fellows and Masons, and their generally anti-Catholic tendencies, and so he refused permission and suggested they revise their constitution based upon that of the St. Vincent de Paul Society. The organization was eventually formed in Boston and was a mainstay at public parades and other celebrations.

Pictured here is the Knights of Columbus Building in Somerville, Massachusetts. The Knights of Columbus were established in New Haven, Connecticut, in 1882, and 10 years later, they appeared in Boston with the founding of the Bunker Hill Council. The Massachusetts State Council was established on April 24, 1894.

Here, Cardinal O'Connell stands in front of the Knights of Columbus Building at Fort Devens, Massachusetts, in 1918, a year after it was established. The Knights of Columbus played a central role in supporting armed forces during World War I. At this building, members sold candy, coffee, tobacco, and other luxuries to soldiers and provided a place for recreational needs.

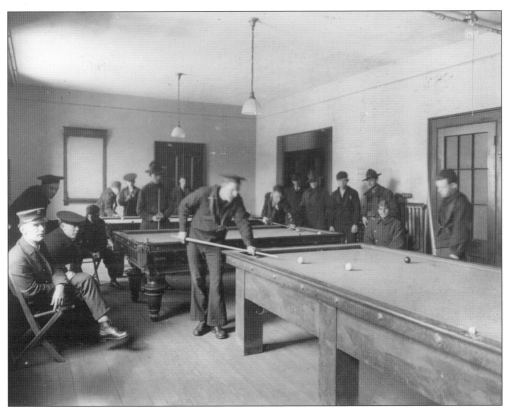

Of the several Knights of Columbus sites in Massachusetts, perhaps the most impressive was the Home for Soldiers and Sailors, also known as "Liberty House," located at 204 Berkeley Street, Boston. It opened on October 27, 1918, and its motto was "Everybody Welcome and Everything Free." In the above photograph, servicemen take a break from their daily responsibilities to play billiards. Below are women volunteers making fresh donuts for the soldiers at the home and those stationed throughout Massachusetts. The Knights of Columbus were called upon again during World War II, by which time they had a new location, the Servicemen's Clubhouse, at 36 Commonwealth Avenue in Boston. (Both, courtesy of Knights of Columbus Museum, New Haven, Connecticut.)

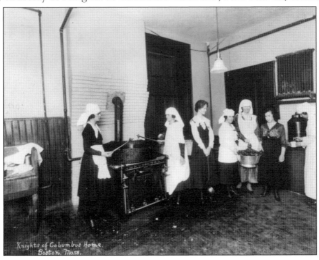

Pictured here, Catholic War Veterans march through the city of Boston and make their way to the Blessed Sacrament Chapel in the Cathedral of the Holy Cross, where they would celebrate Mass with Cardinal Cushing. World War I veterans who attended the Immaculate Conception Church in Brooklyn formed the national association of Catholic War Veterans in May 1935. The founder, Msgr. Edward Higgins, had an audience with Pius XI later that month and received his blessing to form such an organization. In July 1940, the group was officially recognized as a veterans' organization by the federal government. (Both, courtesy of *The Pilot*.)

Five

An International Community

In this undated photograph, Cardinal Cushing meets Madame Chiang Kai-Shek, wife of the Chinese Nationalist leader Chiang Kai-Shek. The meeting takes place at the Boston Symphony Hall; standing beside them is Gov. Leverett Saltonstall, governor of Massachusetts from 1939 to 1945. Like most communities, one cannot think of Boston Catholics as an isolated group. Many immigrated from other countries, welcomed guests from afar, or traveled abroad to broaden their faith.

Throughout its history, Boston has been the destination for immigrants from around the world. While never in great numbers, one of the earliest groups of Catholic immigrants to arrive were from Germany. This community, after much struggle, founded the first "ethnic parish," Holy Trinity, on Suffolk Street (now Shawmut Avenue) in Boston in 1844. Parishes such as this allowed newcomers to worship in their native language and continue to observe customs and traditions from their homeland and, in doing so, helped preserve them for future generations. The parish is also credited with establishing one of the oldest parochial schools, Holy Trinity Grammar School (below), established the same year as the parish. By the late 19th century, the already modest number of German immigrants arriving slowed considerably, and in the mid- to late 19th century, many immigrants moved from the city to other parts of the country for the readily available farmland.

Many French-speaking Catholics, largely originating from Canada, settled in the Merrimack Valley in northeastern Massachusetts starting in the mid-19th century. To help serve this population, Archbishop Williams called upon the Oblates of Mary Immaculate, based in Montreal. In 1868, they established two parishes in Lowell, the French-speaking St. Joseph and the English-speaking Immaculate Conception. At the time, there were about 1,200 French-speaking Catholics in the city, but by 1896, when they replaced St. Joseph with the Church of St. John the Baptist, there were about 20,000.

Taken from North Square in Boston's crowded North End, this photograph shows Sacred Heart (middle of three buildings to the right) and St. John School (left of the church). The parish formed to serve Italian Catholics residing in the neighborhood who desired a place to practice Catholicism in the fashion they were accustomed. It was established by the Scalabrini Fathers, who arrived in 1888, founding the Sacred Heart Chapel, located on Beverly Street, before moving to this site on North Square. The church was constructed in 1833 and was used as a Protestant church, but as the neighborhood became predominantly Catholic, it was purchased and dedicated as Sacred Heart Catholic Church on May 25, 1890. Over the ensuing two decades, renovations would be made to accommodate the growing number of Italian Catholics residing in the neighborhood. In 1912, Cardinal O'Connell purchased the adjacent school building and donated it to the Scalabrini Fathers, who called upon the Sisters of St. Joseph to staff it.

Here, a parade of the Italian Catholic community ends at Our Lady of Perpetual Help, in Boston's Roxbury neighborhood, on September 20, 1926. Including those in the North End, there were 13 parishes in Boston and the surrounding area that identified as Italian. Many of the Italian parishes were established in the first two decades of the 20th century, when immigration from Italy was at its peak.

Archbishop Cushing is pictured with a group of Irish dancers. As various groups of Catholics arrived in Boston, they brought with them a variety of cultures and traditions from their native countries. This is an example of one native tradition that has been passed on for generations and, no doubt, provided an activity in which people who shared the same background could partake in.

In the late 1860s, Lithuanians, many of them Catholic, were known to have started immigrating to the United States. As the Irish had decades before, they left because of famine in their home country. For a number of years, the country was closely tied with Poland, but toward the end of the century, there was a new surge of nationalistic pride in distinctly Lithuanian culture. This saw the community establish uniquely Lithuanian parishes, such as the Immaculate Conception, Cambridge, which was founded in 1910. Above, a class of students receiving First Holy Communion pose for the camera on June 8, 1924. Pictured below are communicants on May 31, 1925.

On Friday, November 19, 1948, the USS *General Bundy*, an Army transport, arrives with 800 passengers categorized as displaced persons, 381 of them Catholic. The group was largely made up of Poles, Czechs, Lithuanians, and Ukrainians who had been victims of political or religious persecution; they represented a small fraction of the estimated 825,000 people displaced from their homes after World War II. At the harbor to meet them were members of the Archdiocese of Boston, including the Msgr. Walter J. Furlong, chancellor; Fr. James H. Doyle, director of the Boston Catholic Charitable Bureau; and Fr. Stanislaus T. Sypek, director of Cambridge Catholic Charitable Bureau. For some, this would not be their last stop as many would continue to other regions of the country for settlement. Many of those arriving were well educated, and the War Relief Services, part of the National Catholic Welfare Council, had arranged jobs for them prior to their arrival.

Polish Catholics hosted a very special visitor, Card. Karol Wojtyla, archbishop of Krakow, Poland, who visited briefly in September 1969. Better known as Pope John Paul II (1978 to 2005), Cardinal Wojtyla had been archbishop of Krakow since 1958 and was appointed a cardinal several months prior to this visit. Above, he stands alongside Cardinal Cushing, with whom he celebrated Mass at St. Adalbert, a Polish parish in Boston's Hyde Park neighborhood, followed by a reception at the new parish center. Below, he greets US military veterans. (Above, courtesy of *The Pilot*.)

Pictured here, a Ukrainian Children's Choir performs at the Peabody Playhouse on Sunday, November 21, 1948. Most Ukrainians are Eastern, rather than Latin, Catholics and were known to have congregated at Holy Trinity, the German church on Shawmut Avenue, Boston, around 1913. Shortly afterward, two Ukrainian parishes formed, St. John the Baptist, Salem, and Christ the King in Boston's Jamaica Plain neighborhood.

In September 1959, during the tense days of the Cold War, Nikita Kruschev toured the United States. Though he would not stop in Boston, the whole nation anxiously followed his journey. Here, Bostonians gather to pray at the Bunker Hill Monument on September 19. (Courtesy of *The Pilot*.)

Cardinal Cushing led a number of pilgrimages abroad while archbishop of Boston, joining Boston Catholics on trips to Rome, the Vatican, and various shrines throughout Europe. Above, the TSS *Olympia* carried pilgrims from Boston, Chicago, New York, and other parts of the United States across the Atlantic Ocean. This was the third year in a row a pilgrimage was taken during the Easter season, and as this was a jubilee year, the trip would be particularly special. Below, Cardinal Cushing can be seen carrying a large wooden cross as he leads Boston pilgrims through St. Peter's Square, toward St. Paul's Basilica. (Above, courtesy of *The Pilot*.)

— HIS EXCELLENCY ARCHBISHOP R.J. CUSHING'S PILGRIMAGE LOURDES —
1954

Above, Archbishop Cushing leads another group of Boston pilgrims to Europe in 1954, which was declared a Marian year by Pope Pius XII and called for special study, devotion, and contemplation to be given to the Blessed Virgin. The pilgrims are posing in front of Our Lady of the Immaculate Conception Church, built on the spot where the Blessed Virgin Mary appeared near Lourdes, France, in 1858. At right is a photograph from the 1956 pilgrimage to Germany. With an additional pilgrimage in 1958, it would make eight pilgrimages in 10 years.

93

From April 19 to 23, 1953, the Boston Garden hosted the World Mission Exhibit. It gave religious orders, clubs, and other organizations that supported missions around the world an opportunity to share their work with the public. The highlight of the event was an address by Bishop Fulton Sheen, director of the National Society for the Propagation of the Faith, the World Mission Exhibit's sponsor. Bishop Sheen would serve as bishop of Rochester, New York, from 1966 until his retirement in 1969. He was well known for his missionary work, radio broadcasts, and television series *Life is Worth Living*. (Above, courtesy of the Office of the Propagation of the Faith, Boston; below, courtesy of *The Pilot*.)

Six

BOSTON CHURCHES, CHAPELS, AND SHRINES

Pictured is a May procession by children of the Gate of Heaven Parish, South Boston. The Gate of Heaven Church, located at the corner of Fourth and I Streets, was dedicated on March 19, 1863. Initially a mission of SS. Peter and Paul, the first Catholic church in South Boston (established 1844), it became an independent parish on January 22, 1866, under the direction of Fr. James F. Sullivan.

Shown here are images from a May procession by children of the Most Holy Redeemer Parish, East Boston. May processions would begin at a local church, and young children, dressed in white, would process alongside a large statue of the Blessed Virgin Mary through the streets of the parish. Returning to the church, the statue would be crowned with a chaplet of flowers while parishioners sang hymns. Below, boys from the Fitton School Cadets march along while guarding the statue of the Blessed Virgin Mary. The original Fitton Grammar School and High School were completed in 1893 and named in honor of the parish's first pastor, Fr. James Fitton.

Known as one of Cardinal Cushing's "workmen's chapels," Our Lady of the Railways, located within Boston's South Station, is pictured under construction. Cardinal Cushing hoped to make the Catholic Church more accessible to people in their everyday lives, and so he constructed this chapel, which was near or on the way to many people's employers. During his tenure as archbishop, Cardinal Cushing would build approximately 80 chapels in a variety of locations, including in hospitals, schools, and shopping malls.

The first Mass at Our Lady of the Railways was celebrated on February 21, 1955. Despite its popularity, the chapel was demolished on September 27, 1972, during renovations. Fortunately, other workmen's chapels have avoided this fate, such as Our Lady of Good Voyage, South Boston, rebuilt in 2017; St. Francis Chapel in the Prudential Center; and Our Lady of the Airways at Boston Logan International Airport, East Boston.

Archbishop Cushing dedicates another one of his workmen's chapels, Our Lady of the Airways, at Boston Logan International Airport, on January 2, 1952. Its purpose was to serve airport workers, airline staff, and travelers passing through. Today, it continues to offer Mass and serves as a place of worship for all faiths.

Here, a few lone Catholics pray in the chapel on Boston Harbor's Long Island in 1938. This late-19th-century chapel was first built to serve the almshouse that existed and continued to see use as over 20 structures were constructed, including a hospital and homeless shelter. The chapel seen here was replaced with the Our Lady of Hope Chapel in 1958.

Boston's Back Bay neighborhood was largely inhabited by Protestants, but in 1887, a reluctant Archbishop Williams finally purchased property there for a Catholic church. He appointed Fr. Richard J. Barry its first pastor, and he celebrated Mass in a temporary chapel set up at the Mechanics Building. The parishioners were largely Irish maids who worked in the homes of wealthy Protestants nearby, but they were remarkably generous supporting the parish and helped found St. Cecilia Church, dedicated on April 22, 1894. The Catholic population in the neighborhood quickly outgrew the church, and two missions were later established in the area. The first was St. Ann, in the Back Bay neighborhood of Boston, at the corner of St. Stephen and Gainsborough Streets. The former Episcopal Church of the Messiah, erected in 1892, was purchased by Cardinal O'Connell in 1928 and dedicated on October 28 of that year. It was later referred to as the "University Parish," serving the Catholics attending the city's many colleges and universities.

Here, a crowd gathers outside of St. Clement Church, Boston, the second mission originally attached to St. Cecilia. Located at the corner of Boylston and Ipswich Streets, this beautiful Gothic stone church was built in 1926 as the Universalist Church of the Redemption, but with its congregation unable to sustain it, it was purchased by Cardinal O'Connell and made a mission of St. Cecilia. It was dedicated as St. Clement Catholic Church on December 8, 1935. Its role has changed several times in the ensuing decades. On May 3, 1945, Archbishop Cushing rededicated it as the Eucharistic Shrine of Perpetual Adoration and appointed the Franciscan Missionaries of Mary as its caretakers. From that time to the late 1960s, there were always two sisters kneeling in silent adoration of the Blessed Sacrament. By that time, the construction of the Massachusetts Turnpike uprooted the neighborhood, and attendance declined. In 1976, its fortunes changed as the Oblates of the Virgin Mary became caretakers, opening a seminary there two years later, and in 2009, perpetual adoration commenced once more.

Here, crowds gather for the dedication of the bells of Our Lady of Perpetual Help, in Boston's Roxbury neighborhood, on July 3, 1910. Also known as the "Mission Church" or "Basilica," it was established by priests of the Most Holy Redeemer, or Redemptorists, who arrived at the invitation of Fr. James Augustine Healy in May 1869 to establish a mission at his parish, St. James, in Boston. With early success, he soon petitioned Archbishop Williams to allow them to establish a permanent mission, and in September 1869, they purchased land in Roxbury, then known as Boston Highlands, called Franklin Gardens. The first church on the property was completed on April 7, 1878, and five years later, it would become its own parish. This parish is also significant as many of its priests to this day serve as chaplains to the hospitals in the Longwood Medical Area.

In recognition of the Marian Year declared by Pope Pius XII, approximately 2,500 Boston priests gathered from September 6 to 8, 1954, at Our Lady of Perpetual Help. The first two days started with participants assembling at the Mission Church Grammar School before processing into the church where they celebrated Mass with Archbishop Cushing. Marian Year observances also included Benediction and Exposition of the Blessed Sacrament.

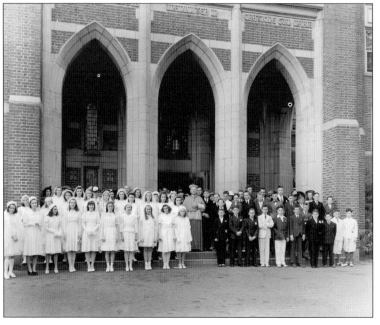

A confirmation class poses outside of the Cenacle Convent, in Boston's Brighton neighborhood, around 1940. The convent was one of the earliest retreat houses for women in the city and was operated by the Sisters of Our Lady of the Cenacle, who purchased the site at the corner of Lake and Kenrick Streets in 1909. The sisters arrived the following year and opened it to the public on May 19, 1912.

Pictured here is a group of converts in front of Blessed Sacrament Mission Center, in the Roxbury neighborhood of Boston, shortly after receiving the sacrament of First Holy Communion on June 9, 1934. The mission center, located at 60 Vernon Street, was overseen by the Sisters of the Blessed Sacrament, who were sent by St. Katharine Drexel 20 years earlier to serve the black Catholic community in Boston. Upon their arrival, they opened St. Joseph Mission, but the chapel proved too small, and for a time, they used the old St. Patrick Church. St. Katharine Drexel was present at the dedication of the mission center on December 16, 1934. It remained open until 1967, when it was claimed by eminent domain and became the site for Madison Park High School.

Pictured here are the Archbishop Cushing Cadets, later renamed the Cardinal Cushing Cadets, an all-girl drum and bugle corps composed of children from the Blessed Sacrament Mission Center on Vernon Street. From 1949 through 1956, they earned the title of best all-girl drum and bugle corps in the Archdiocese of Boston in competitions hosted by the Catholic Youth Organization.

In this undated photograph, parishioners file out of St. Andrew the Apostle, located in Boston's Forest Hills neighborhood. Parishioners attended St. Thomas Aquinas, Jamaica Plain, until St. Andrew's was formed as a separate parish in 1918, first meeting in Minton Hall on Forest Hills Square. Construction of the church seen here began in the summer of 1919, and the first Mass was celebrated there on September 11, 1921.

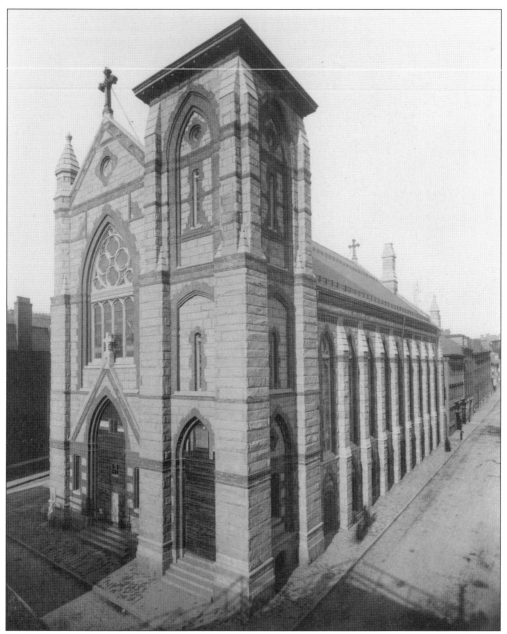

Established in 1828, St. Mary, Charlestown, was the first parish in the neighborhood. It was the second church built in the Boston area, after the Cathedral of the Holy Cross on Franklin Street, and would be the only parish in that part of the city for nearly 30 years. After that time, St. Francis de Sales was constructed to serve the north half of Charlestown, with St. Mary serving the southern part of the city, which was annexed to Boston in 1872. Even with another church in the area, the original building on Richmond (now Rutherford) Street still could not accommodate the large number of parishioners, which prompted the parish to construct a new home for itself, pictured here. Made of granite in the Tudor Gothic style, the church was dedicated on October 2, 1892. The original church building remained until it was demolished nine years later, in 1901.

Pictured here is St. Joseph Church, in Boston's West End, which was almost completely demolished during a period of urban renewal in the mid-20th century. The church was purchased by the parish in 1862 and renovated in 1902. It was one of the few structures left standing. Note the parishioners stumbling through the rubble to attend Mass in 1962. Just to the right and behind the church

stands the Museum of Science, built the decade before. In the late 1960s, the lower church was converted to a parish hall, and further renovations were made to conform to the Second Vatican Council. The church reopened in 1974. (Courtesy of the West End Museum, Boston.)

Pictured here is the original St. Patrick Church, Roxbury, which was located on Northampton Street in Boston's South End. The church served St. Patrick parish from its establishment in 1836, but in 1874, the parish would be relocated to Roxbury, where it is still active today. Since that time, the church building has been used for a variety of purposes, including by the Sisters of the Blessed Sacrament.

Here, a crowd gathers at the cathedral on June 30, 1947, for the Episcopal ordination of Bishop John J. Wright as auxiliary bishop of Boston. At this time, the city was home to dozens of Catholic churches and schools, and more would continue to pop up as the community grew.

Seven

THE EXTENDED CATHOLIC COMMUNITY

It would be a disservice to view Catholic Boston in isolation from the surrounding cities and towns and the people who reside there. The following images depict examples of the vibrant Catholic life that exists outside of the city itself. Here, Cardinal Cushing blesses a fishing fleet in Gloucester, Massachusetts, on June 28, 1964.

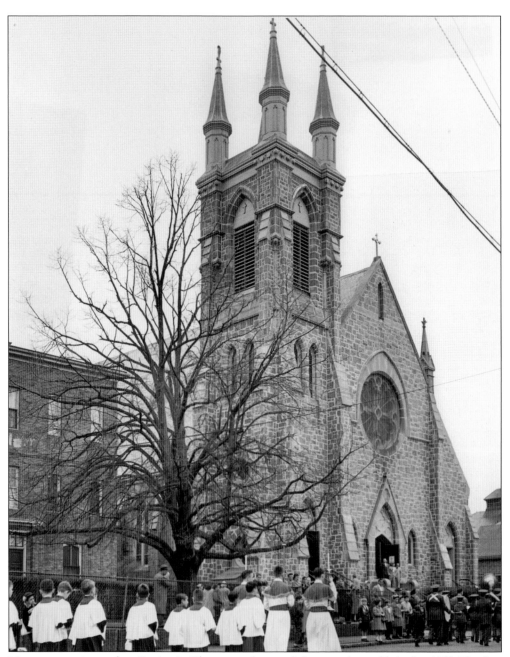

Here, a procession ends at St. Ann's, Gloucester, the town's first parish, established in 1855. The first Catholic Mass was celebrated in the town in 1849. Later, a former Baptist church was purchased for the parish and moved to a new site, dedicated on September 30, 1855. The church was called the "Fishermen's Church" by John Boyle O'Reilly, editor of *The Pilot*, its mission being to serve the fishing community based in the town. In more perilous times, it was thought essential that a fisherman have a regular pastor to confess to before seaborne voyages in case he did not return. This parish is also known for having many missions that later developed into parishes, including St. Joachim, Rockport, and St. John the Baptist, Essex. Dedicated on July 31, 1881, the church seen here replaced the repurposed Baptist church.

Pictured here is the Blessed Sacrament Church, Saugus, which provides an excellent example of what an early church may have looked like. Many early church buildings were purchased from other Christian denominations. With the financial support and manual labor of parishioners, some parishes were able to construct a new church at the start. Often, these early churches were made of wood due to its affordability and the ease and speed with which it could be constructed. This particular church was dedicated on October 30, 1898, while still a mission of Sacred Heart, Lynn. Sadly, it burned down on January 25, 1909, and was replaced by a stone church whose basement chapel opened one year later; however, the remainder of the structure stalled. Blessed Sacrament became a parish in 1917, and a new church was finally completed in 1950.

St. Mary, Quincy, was the first Catholic parish established on the South Shore, the area between Boston and Cape Cod, in 1842. Like many parishes in the 19th century, the pastor of this one church would often be responsible for serving Catholics in a large area comprising several towns. Before churches were constructed, Mass would often be held in a private home or public building while a priest was visiting.

Above, cars are parked in a vacant lot across from St. Catherine of Alexandria, located in the Graniteville section of Westford, on April 18, 1937. The towns of Westford and Tyngsborough were initially missions of St. John the Evangelist, Chelmsford. A small church was constructed at Graniteville in 1892, and in June 1922, it was named an independent parish, with Fr. Aloysius S. Malone as its pastor.

Pictured here is an event at Our Lady of the Assumption Church, Chelsea. The first parish established in Chelsea was St. Rose of Lima in 1848, which still exists today. The Society of Mary, better known as the Marists, arrived in the area and petitioned for a separate church to serve the French-speaking population in the town, which was granted to them. On May 5, 1907, the French-speaking Catholics met in the basement of the St. Rose of Lima School for Mass, and by the following year, they were able to build a small basement church on Broadway. This mission of Our Lady of the Assumption was elevated to its own parish in 1912. In 1924, work began to build an upper church over the basement church; once completed, it was dedicated on November 29, 1925.

During the mid-18th century, Lowell was probably the city whose Catholic population grew the most after Boston. A small Catholic community started to form in the preceding decades as people migrated there to find work. The earliest recorded visit by a Catholic priest was in 1822 by Fr. Patrick Byrne, followed by Fr. John Mahoney, of Salem, in 1827. The latter would serve as the first pastor of what came to be St. Patrick Parish, and several years later, the first church was dedicated on July 3, 1831. The congregation outgrew St. Patrick, and so a new church was built, opening on October 29, 1853. The new church served the community until it burned down on January 11, 1904. The image here of the current St. Patrick was dedicated November 18, 1906.

Within a decade of St. Patrick Parish being established, the burgeoning Catholic population in Lowell necessitated the construction of a second parish, St. Peter, which was established in 1841. The first pastor, Fr. James Conway, settled the parish in a church on the corner of Gorham and Appleton Streets, pictured above. Its dedication ceremony was on October 16, 1842. In 1890, however, the property was sold to the US government for a post office, and the congregation bought land farther down Gorham Street for a new granite church (pictured at right), designed by Patrick Keely. It was dedicated on May 10, 1903.

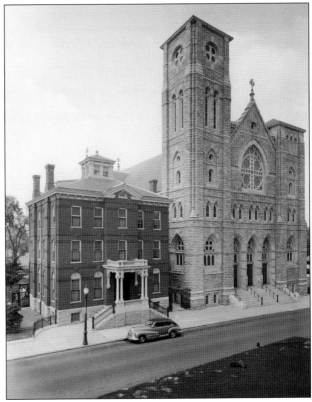

St. Marie, Lowell, was formed after a petition for a new parish was submitted by the residents of South Lowell. In 1906, under the direction of the Oblates of Mary Immaculate, the parish opened its own school and chapel designated a mission of St. Joseph, Lowell. By 1925, the members built a new church, and in late 1931, parishioners were informed they were no longer a mission but an independent parish. This church was razed in 1968 due to the construction of Interstate 495, which cut through the church property. Shown here are the church (above) and school (below) in 1936.

The real-photo postcard above was taken from the front of steps of St. Patrick Church, Lowell, as thousands gather in anticipation of Cardinal O'Connell's arrival for the dedication of the Cardinal O'Connell Parkway on November 17, 1918. The day's events included a parade of military and Catholic organizations and the dedication of a granite fountain with the bust of Cardinal O'Connell, which was unveiled by his niece Josephine O'Connell.

Pictured here are photographs from the laying of the cornerstone for St. Catherine of Siena, Norwood, on April 4, 1909. In the crowd, one can see the arrival of Bishop John Brady, who had the honor of laying the cornerstone on this special occasion. Bishop Brady was born in Ireland in 1842 and ordained in Dublin on December 5, 1864. During his lifetime, he served at St. Vincent de Paul, South Boston; Immaculate Conception, Newburyport; and St. Joseph, Amesbury. He was the first auxiliary bishop of Boston from August 5, 1891, until his death on January 6, 1910. In the early 20th century, the demand for Catholic parishes still outweighed the rate at which they could be established, and events such as this often drew thousands of spectators.

Here are more photographs from the cornerstone being laid at St. Catherine of Siena, Norwood. This parish is typical of how the Catholic community developed in suburban towns. Norwood was originally part of Dedham, referred to as "South Dedham," but was formally incorporated as a separate town in 1872. Since 1863, the town's Catholics met at a Universalist meetinghouse and were served by priests from St. Mary, Dedham, until this church was completed in 1910. Norwood was declared an independent parish in 1922.

Pictured here are, from left to right, Fr. Francis L Keenan, pastor of St. Michael Church; Rev. Raymond S. Hall, from St. John Episcopal Church; Albert Davis, a Civil War veteran; Mayor George T. Ashe; Dudley L. Page, department commander of the Grand Army of the Republic; and Alexander D. Mitchell, chief marshal of the parade and a Spanish-American War veteran. They pose together during a Memorial Day celebration in Lowell, Massachusetts, May 30, 1940.

Even before the Catholic Youth Organization had been formed, sports were a major part of Catholic life, offering Catholics the chance to come together and compete against their neighboring parishes and schools. Pictured here is the first baseball team from Our Lady Help of Christians Church, Newton, which formed in 1927.

The unique architecture of the Sacred Heart Church, Groton, can be attributed to its origins as an Episcopal chapel. Constructed in 1887 and named St. John Chapel, it served Dr. Endicott Peabody's famous Groton School for boys. As enrollment increased, it was enlarged in 1891, but it was then left unused when a new stone church was completed in 1900. The Catholic population of Groton had been a mission of St. Mary's, Ayer, since 1890, and celebrated Mass in an abandoned schoolhouse. Desperate for a church of their own, their prayers were answered when they were given the chapel, and in September 1904, the congregation moved the building into town on rollers. It was blessed the following month, and in 1907, it was established as an independent parish under the leadership of Fr. Charles A. Finnegan. It is pictured here in 1938.

St. Catherine of Genoa was the third parish in Somerville established to serve the western part of town. Land was purchased on Summer Street on November 17, 1891, and parishioners gathered in an old, wooden building on the site to celebrate their first Mass together on April 17, 1892, Easter Sunday. Interestingly, the first pastor, Fr. James J. O'Brien, was the son of former Boston mayor Hugh O'Brien. The wooden church sustained the parish until plans for a grander one were formed, the result of which would be the church pictured here. The cornerstone was laid on June 6, 1908, and the lower church was completed the following June. The upper portion of the church took much longer, and the first Mass was not celebrated in that space until April 4, 1920, again Easter Sunday. In the 1920s, the parish would also establish a school, named the Little Flower Elementary School after St. Teresa of Lisieux and staffed by the Sisters of St. Joseph.

The Sacred Heart of Jesus, Cambridge, is perhaps most notable for the publication the *Sacred Heart Review*, published weekly from 1888 to 1918. Fr. John O'Brien founded this parish newspaper, and its readership grew as he incorporated news from outside of the parish, achieving a national audience. By 1895, it had grown too large for one person to oversee, and so the Review Publishing Company was formed, comprised of about 100 New England priests. Above is an undated photograph of the paper's printing office. Below, a crowd gathers outside of the Sacred Heart Church on "Come Home Sunday," November 26, 1950, welcoming back former parishioners.

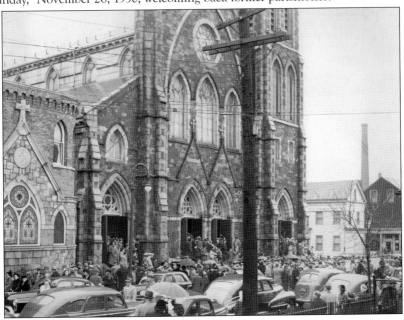

Those living in North Cambridge were served by St. Peter Church, Cambridge, established in 1848. Land was purchased on Spruce Street (now Rindge Avenue) in 1890 and 1891, and a three-story brick building was constructed with a chapel on the first floor and classrooms on the other two. It became a mission of St. Peter, and the first Mass was held at the chapel on February 28, 1892. Less than a year later, this small mission would be named an independent parish, and by 1905, construction began on a new church to accommodate the growing number of parishioners. The parish would also build a parochial grammar school in 1913 and high school in 1921. Tragedy struck when the church was destroyed in a 1956 fire, but immediately after, efforts were made to rebuild it, and the project was completed in 1962.

The parish in Hopkinton was established on June 30, 1866. Mass was held at a small church named St. Malachy, but in 1876, work began on a more impressive Gothic church that would not be completed until its dedication on September 2, 1889. The new church was named St. John the Evangelist, pictured here, and was constructed on one of the highest spots in town, on Church Street.

Pictured here, parishioners from the Blessed Sacrament Parish, Cambridge, pose in their costumes from a performance of the *Passion of Christ*. Passion plays depict the final days in the life of Jesus Christ, starting with his arrival in Jerusalem, his trial and conviction, and ultimately his crucifixion, death, and resurrection.

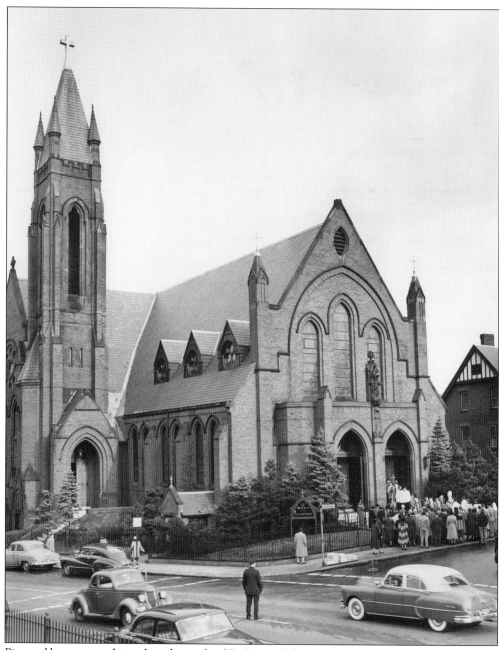

Pictured here, a crowd is gathered outside of St. Mary of the Assumption, Brookline, as the parish celebrates its 100th anniversary in 1952. It marks the occasion of the first Mass celebrated in the Brookline Lyceum on July 30, 1852. The following year, the parish was able to celebrate Mass in a church on Christmas Day 1853, but the building fell victim to a fire in 1855, and it was not until August 22, 1886, that a new church at the corner of Linden Place and Harvard Street was dedicated. In 1899, the parish opened its own school, staffed by the Sisters of Notre Dame de Namur, in the church's basement. Eight years later saw the opening of a separate school building, and in 1924, a new high school was created to serve the Brookline community.

This c. 1921 photograph shows the Immaculate Conception Brigade marching. It was comprised of parishioners from Immaculate Conception, Malden. The parish has been in existence since 1854, and at times during the 19th century, it encompassed the towns of Malden, Medford, Stoneham, Wakefield, Reading, and part of Everett.

Upon his death, Cardinal Cushing's body was laid to rest in the Portiuncula Chapel in Hanover, Massachusetts. The chapel is a replica of St. Francis's Chapel in Assisi and is located on the grounds of the Cardinal Cushing School and Training Center, a school and residence founded in 1947 to aid mentally disabled children. At the time of this writing, the campus is home to the headquarters of the Cardinal Cushing Centers.

DISCOVER THOUSANDS OF LOCAL HISTORY BOOKS FEATURING MILLIONS OF VINTAGE IMAGES

Arcadia Publishing, the leading local history publisher in the United States, is committed to making history accessible and meaningful through publishing books that celebrate and preserve the heritage of America's people and places.

Find more books like this at
www.arcadiapublishing.com

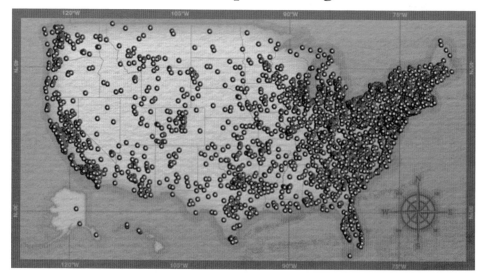

Search for your hometown history, your old stomping grounds, and even your favorite sports team.